SELECTED BY
BARBARA ROGASKY

PHOTOGRAPHS BY
MARC TAUSS

SCHOLASTIC PRESS
NEW YORK

leaf

by leaf

autumn poems

ISBN 0-590-25347-6

LIBRARY OF CONGRESS CATALOGING-IN-PUBLICATION DATA

Leaf by leaf: autumn poems / selected by Barbara Rogasky ;
photography by Marc Tauss.— 1st ed.   p.   cm.
1. Autumn—Juvenile poetry. 2. Children's poetry, American.
3. Children's poetry, English. [1. Autumn—Poetry.
2. Autumn poetry—Collections. 3. English poetry—Collections.]
I. Rogasky, Barbara. II. Tauss, Marc ill.
PS595.A89 A9 2001 811.008'033—dc21 00-046997
12 11 10 9 8 7 6 5 4 3 2 1   01 02 03 04 05
Printed in Singapore   46

First edition, September 2001

The photographs in this book were shot with large
format, medium format, and handmade cameras.
Special thanks to Paul Colin for his invaluable assistance.

The text type was set in Futura Bold.
Art direction and design by Marijka Kostiw

To Anna Janney DeArmond

— B.R.

This book is dedicated to Marijka

for her never-ending support,

to my parents Nadine and Jack,

to Ian, Karen and Dylan,

and the loving memory of my uncle,

Charles Tauss.

— M.T.

table of contents

september

The golden-rod is yellow;
    The corn is turning brown;
The trees in apple orchards
    With fruit are bending down.

The gentian's bluest fringes
    Are curling in the sun;
In dusky pods the milkweed
    Its hidden silk has spun.

The sedges flaunt their harvest
    In every meadow nook;
And asters by the brookside
    Make asters in the brook.

From dewy lanes at morning
    The grapes' sweet odors rise;
At noon the roads all flutter
    With golden butterflies.

By all these lovely tokens
    September days are here,
With summer's best of weather,
    And autumn's best of cheer.

— HELEN HUNT JACKSON

hymn to intellectual beauty

The day becomes more solemn and serene
    When noon is past—there is a harmony
    In autumn, and a lustre in its sky,
Which through the summer is not heard or seen,
As if it could not be, as if it had not been!

— PERCY BYSSHE SHELLEY

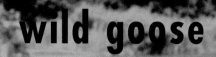

wild goose

He climbs the wind above
green clouds of pine,
Honking to hail the
gathering migration.
And, arching toward the
south, pulls to align
His flight into the great
spearhead formation.

He'll find a bayou land of
hidden pools,
And bask amid lush fern
and water lily
Far from the frozen world
of earth-bound fools
Who, shivering, maintain
that geese are silly.

— CURTIS HEATH

FROM
james lee

Ah, love, but a day,
  And the world has changed!
The sun's away,
  And the bird's estranged;
The wind has dropped,
  And the sky's deranged:
Summer has stopped.

— *ROBERT BROWNING*

the chipmunk's day

In and out the bushes, up the ivy
Into the hole
By the old oak stump, the chipmunk flashes.
Up the pole

To the feeder full of seeds he dashes,
Stuffs his cheeks,
The chickadee and titmouse scold him.
Down he streaks.

. . .

Down the path,
Home to his warm hole stuffed with sweet
Things to eat.
Neat and slight and shining, his front feet

Curled at his breast, he sits there while the sun
Stripes the red west
With its last light:
The chipmunk
Dives to his rest.

— RANDALL JARRELL

the sheaves

Where long the shadows of the wind had rolled,
Green wheat was yielding to the change assigned;
And as by some vast magic undivined
The world was turning slowly into gold.
. . .
Fair days went on till on another day
A thousand golden sheaves were lying there,
Shining and still, but not for long to stay—
As if a thousand girls with golden hair
Might rise from where they slept and go away.

— EDWIN ARLINGTON ROBINSON

london voluntaries

For earth and sky and air
Are golden everywhere,
And golden with a gold so suave and fine
The looking on it lifts the heart like wine.
— WILLIAM ERNEST HENLEY

FROM
autumn evening

. . . A heron flew over

With that remote ridiculous cry, "Quawk," the cry

That seems to make the silence more silent. A dozen

Flops of the wing, a drooping glide, at the end of the glide

The cry, and a dozen flops of the wing,

I watched him pass on the autumn-colored sky; beyond him

Jupiter shone for the evening star.

the alchemist in the city

My window shows the travelling clouds,
Leaves spent, new seasons, alter'd sky,
The making and the melting crowds:
The whole world passes; I stand by.

— *GERARD MANLEY HOPKINS*

lady in grey

broadly smiling
a lady in grey cycles
against the autumn wind

— ARNOLD VERMEEREN

FROM
october

Knuckles of the rain
on the roof,
chuckles into the drain-
pipe, spatters on
the leaves that litter
the grass. . . .

— *MAY SWENSON*

FROM
the bonfire

We raked leaves all the sunny afternoon
into a slim brown row along the hill.
. . .
As we worked on the hazy sky became
more distant, and a Phoenix-wing of flame
flung out across the west. The hill grew dim.
The solitary poplar on its rim,
black, naked, stood alone against the sky.
Its lilac shadow crept, then hastened, ran,
and reached your feet. You wiped your forehead dry
and looked up. "Shall we light them—" I began—
Your match already made a little flare
twin to the star caught in the poplar there,
and one thin smoke-wisp drifted up the air.

— ROBERT PACKARD

the wild swans at coole

The trees are in their autumn beauty,
The woodland paths are dry,
Under the October twilight the water
Mirrors a still sky;
Upon the brimming water among the stones
Are nine-and-fifty swans.

— WILLIAM BUTLER YEATS

23

wind and silver

Greatly shining,
The Autumn moon floats in the thin sky;
And the fish-ponds shake their backs and flash their dragon scales
As she passes over them.

— AMY LOWELL

birds' nests

The summer nests are uncovered by autumn wind,
Some torn, others dislodged, all dark,
Everyone sees them: low or high in a tree,
Or hedge, or single bush, they hang like a mark.

Since there's no need of eyes to see them with
I cannot help but a little shame
That I missed most, even at eye's level, till
The leaves blew off and made the seeing no game.

— EDWARD THOMAS

FROM
come up from the fields father

Lo, 'tis autumn,

Lo, where the trees, deeper green, yellower and redder,

Cool and sweeten Ohio's villages with leaves fluttering in the moderate wind,

Where apples ripe in the orchards hang and grapes on the trellis'd vines,

(Smell you the smell of the grapes on the vines?

Smell you the buckwheat where the bees were lately buzzing?)

Above all, lo, the sky so calm, so transparent after the rain,

and with wondrous clouds,

Below too, all calm, all vital and beautiful, and the farm prospers well.

— WALT WHITMAN

FROM

ulalume

The skies they were ashen and sober;

   The leaves they were crispèd and sere—

   The leaves they were withering and sere;

It was night, in the lonesome October

   Of my most immemorial year;

It was hard by the dim lake of Auber,

   In the misty mid region of Weir—

It was down by the dank tarn of Auber,

   In the ghoul-haunted woodlands of Weir.

          — EDGAR ALLAN POE

november day

Old haggard wind has
    plucked the trees
Like pheasants, held
    between her knees.
In rows she hangs them,
    bare and neat,
Their brilliant plumage at
    her feet.

— *ELEANOR AVERITT*

the great horned owl

How you swoop from the dark of the trees
against the blackest blue sky of the November
full moon, your wings spread wide as my
arms, rough heavy sails rigged for a storm.
The moon blinds me as she glides in ripping
skeins of clouds. On your forehead you bear
her crescents, your eyes hypnotic
as her clock-face disc. . . .

— *MARGE PIERCY*

the window washer

Twenty stories up
In the chill of later November,
Wiping the grime
Off the pane, the many windows

Which have no way of opening—
Windows mirroring the clouds and sea gulls—
That figure who lets light in
Into each stilled interior.

— *CHARLES SIMIC*

city autumn

The air breathes frost. A thin wind beats
Old dust and papers down gray streets
And blows brown leaves with curled-up edges
At frightened sparrows on window ledges.
A snowflake falls like an errant feather:
A vagabond draws his cloak together,
And an old man totters past with a cane
Wondering if he'll see spring again.

— *JOSEPH MONCURE MARCH*

looking for mushrooms

Fall: the dry threshold
To the woods, trees blown apart
Leaf by leaf. A black snake,
Coiled in the sun, flutters
Its forked tongue and glides
Like a stroke of oil over
The path. . . .

— MARY OLIVER

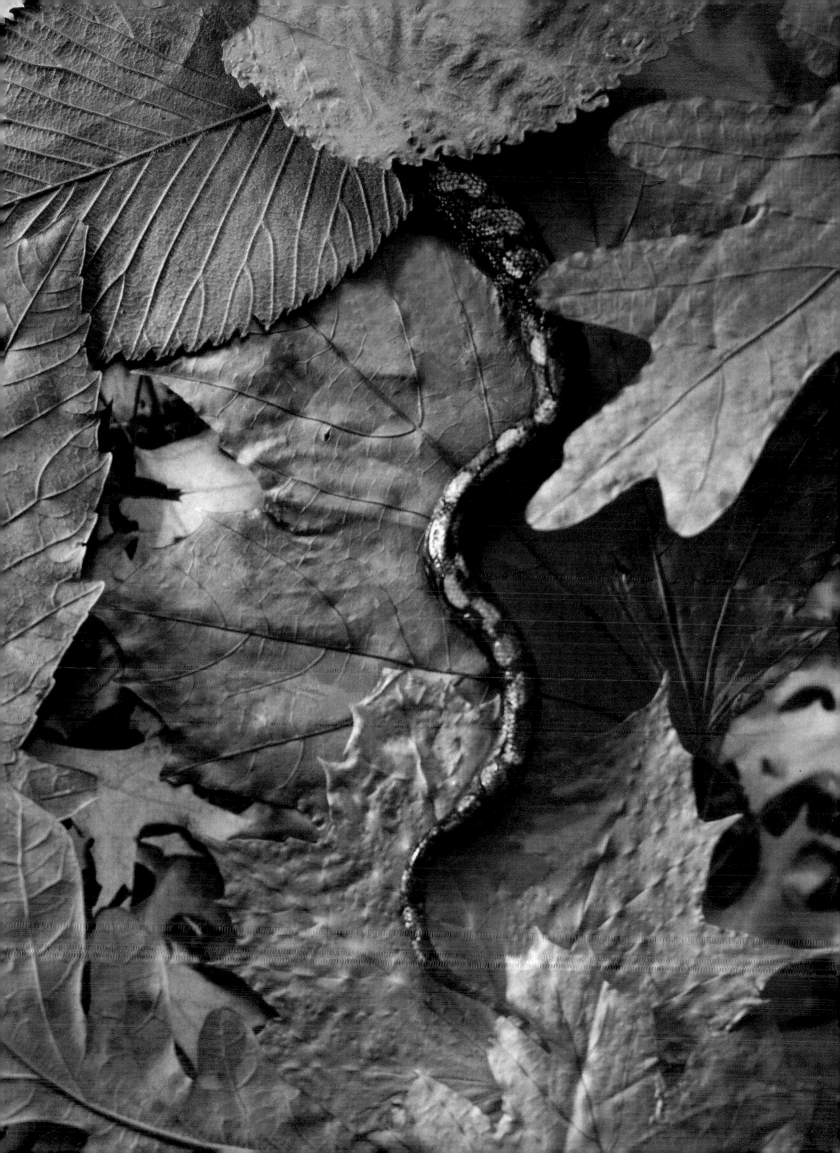

two lives and others

Beyond the fields where crows cawed at a hawk
The road bent down between oaks, pines, and maples:

. . . Moss crunched stiff underfoot, and overhead
The sky was gradually freezing, white across blue.
We hurried our walk through shadows, yet it was
A noticeable sort of afternoon:

. . . Round the next bend to twilight we went past
A solitary house, one room lamplighted,
An old man at supper alone facing the wall.
If he was aware he gave no sign.
We circled home, that last day before snow.

— WINFIELD TOWNLEY SCOTT

the frost

Young man,
Seize every moment
Of your time.
The days fly by;
Ere long you too
Will grow old.

If you believe me not,
See there, in the courtyard,
How the frost
Glitters white and cold and cruel
On the grass
That once was green.

      — *Tzu Yeh*

wild weather

Winter is coming! The wind that blows
Hard from the north, from the land of snows,
Nips the fingers and reddens the nose,
Whips the branches and tugs the clothes
    And strips the tree,
Till nothing is left of her yellow attire;
And hoar frost streaks the choclatey mire,
And crows string like crotchets along the wire,
And wanderers think of home and fire,
    And so do we.

— *SHIRLEY HUGHES*

acknowledgments

Shirley Hughes. "Wild Weather" by Shirley Hughes from *Stories by Firelight*. Reprinted by permission of The Bodley Head/Random House UK.

Randall Jarrell. From "The Chipmunk's Day" by Randall Jarrell. Copyright © 1963, 1965 by Randall Jarrell from the book *The Bat-Poet* published by Michael di Capua Books/HarperCollins Publishers. Permission granted by Rhoda Weyr Agency, NY.

Robinson Jeffers. From "Autumn Evening" by Robinson Jeffers from *Roan Stallion, Tamor and Other Poems* by Robinson Jeffers. Reprinted by permission of Jeffers Literary Properties.

Amy Lowell. From "Wind and Silver" by Amy Lowell from *The Complete Poetical Works of Amy Lowell*. Copyright © 1955 by Houghton Mifflin Company, © renewed 1983 by Houghton Mifflin Company, Brinton P. Roberts and G. D'Andelot Belin, Esq. Reprinted by permission of Houghton Mifflin Co. All rights reserved.

Mary Oliver. From "Looking for Mushrooms" by Mary Oliver from *Twelve Moons* published by Little, Brown and Company, Inc., 1979. Permission granted by Little, Brown and Company, Inc., and Molly Malone Cook Literary Agency.

Marge Piercy. From "The great horned owl" by Marge Piercy from *The Moon Is Always Female* by Marge Piercy. Copyright © 1980 by Marge Piercy. Reprinted by permission of Alfred A. Knopf, Inc., and Wallace Literary Agency.

Charles Simic. From "Window Washer" by Charles Simic. Reprinted by permission of Station Hill Press, Inc.

May Swenson. From "October" by May Swenson from *Nature* by May Swenson. Copyright © 1994 by the Literary Estate of May Swenson. Reprinted by permission of Houghton Mifflin Co. All rights reserved.

Arnold Vermeeren. Haiku, "Lady in Grey" by Arnold P.O.S. Vermeeren from Shiki Internet Haiku Salon Site of October 27, 1996. Reprinted by permission of the author.

W.B. Yeats. From "The Wild Swans at Coole" by W. B. Yeats. Reprinted by permission of A.P. Watt Ltd. on behalf of Michael D. Yeuls.

Tzu Yeh. "The Frost" by Tzu Yeh, from *Poems Of a Hundred Names*, Henry H. Hart, Stanford University Press, 1938. Reprinted by permission of Stanford University Press.

Every effort has been made by the publisher to locate each owner of the copyrighted material reprinted in this book to secure the necessary permissions. If there are any questions regarding the use of these materials, the publisher will take appropriate corrective measures to acknowledge ownership in future editions.